Contents

India

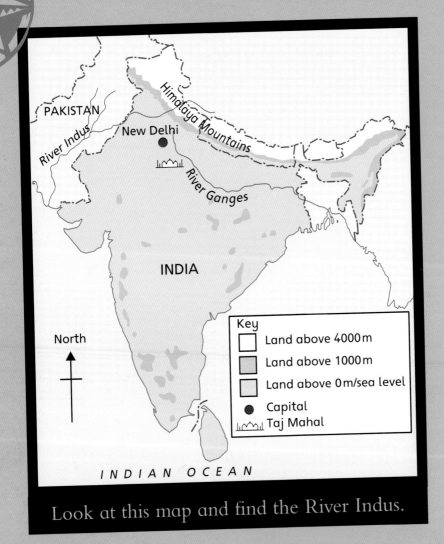

PAKISTAN

River Indus

Himalaya Mountains

New Delhi

River Ganges

INDIA

North

Key
- ☐ Land above 4000m
- ◻ Land above 1000m
- ☐ Land above 0m/sea level
- ● Capital
- ⌂ Taj Mahal

INDIAN OCEAN

Look at this map and find the River Indus.

India takes its name from the River Indus.
This river runs through Pakistan, which
used to be part of India. India is in Asia.
It is shaped like a diamond.

India is almost 13 times bigger than the UK.

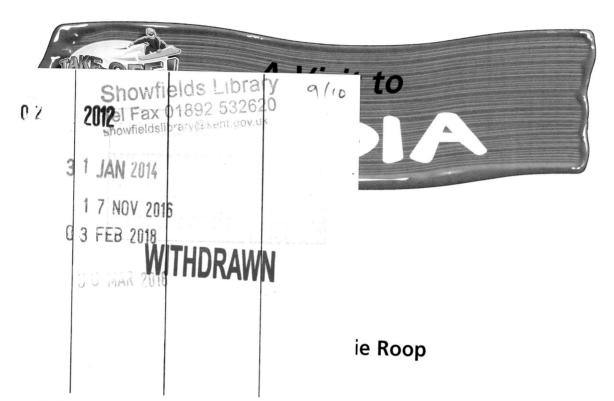

A Visit to

DIA

ie **Roop**

Awarded for excellence
to Arts & Libraries

Kent
County
Council

Heinemann
LIBRARY

First published in Great Britain by Heinemann Library
Halley Court, Jordan Hill, Oxford OX2 8EJ
a division of Reed Educational and Professional Publishing Ltd.
Heinemann is a registered trademark of Reed Educational & Professional Publishing Limited.

OXFORD MELBOURNE AUCKLAND
IBADAN JOHANNESBURG BLANTYRE
GABORONE PORTSMOUTH (NH) USA CHICAGO

Designed by AMR and Celia Floyd
Illustrations by Art Construction
Originated by Dot Gradations, UK
Printed in Hong Kong/China

04 03 02 01
10 9 8 7 6 5 4 3 2

ISBN 0 431 08287 1

This book is also available in hardback (ISBN 0 431 08282 0).

British Library Cataloguing in Publication Data

Roop, Peter
  A visit to India. – (Take-off!)
  1. India – Social conditions – 1947 – – Juvenile literature
  2. India – Geography – Juvenile literature
  3. India – Social life and customs – Juvenile literature
  I.Title II. Roop, Connie III. India
  954'.052

Acknowledgements

The Publishers would like to thank the following for permission to reproduce photographs: J Allan Cash Ltd: pp7, 8, 14, 15, 18, 21, 28, 29; Hutchison Library: J Horner pp10, 23, J Highet p25, L Taylor p22; Images of India: pp13, 27; Magnum: R Raghu pp19, 24; Panos Pictures: S Anwar p6, R Berriedale-Johnson p5, N Durrell-McKenna p12, J Horner p16, Z Nelson p11, D O'Leary pp17, 20, P Smith pp9, 26

Cover photograph reproduced with permission of J. Allan Cash

Our thanks to Sue Graves and Stephanie Byars for their advice and expertise in the preparation of this book.

Every effort has been made to contact copyright holders of any material reproduced in this book. Any omissions will be rectified in subsequent printings if notice is given to the Publisher.

For more information about Heinemann Library books, or to order, please telephone +44 (0)1865 888066, or send a fax to +44 (0)1865 314091. You can visit our website at www.heinemann.co.uk

Any words appearing in bold, **like this**, are explained in the Glossary.

Cities in India are very crowded.

Many people live in India. Only China has more people than India. Most Indians live in the country but the cities are very crowded.

Land

The Himalayan Mountains are the highest in the world.

India has three main types of land. In the north of the country are the Himalayan Mountains. These are the highest mountains in the world.

6

seashore

The Indian peninsula.

The middle of India forms the largest **plain** in the world. The plain is very good for growing **crops** and many people live there. The other part of India is the **peninsula**. It has high, flat mountains and many miles of beautiful seashore.

7

Landmarks

The Taj Mahal was built on the River Jumna.

The Taj Mahal is India's most famous building. It was built 300 years ago. The Taj Mahal was built in memory of a much loved queen, called Mumtaz Mahal.

River Ganges

Hindus pray and bathe in the River Ganges.

The River Ganges is a long wide river. To many Hindus in India, it is a holy river and there are many places along its banks where people pray and wash in it.

The River Ganges is 2510 kilometres long.

Homes

Many people live in flats in this Indian city.

In the cities people live in small flats. Many poor people live in huts or tents or have no homes at all. It is very dangerous for these people in the **monsoon season**.

The monsoon season lasts from June to September.

Many members of the same family all share this small house.

Most people live in country villages. Some homes are made of **bamboo** or home-made clay bricks. Large families live together in one building.

Food

Getting the meal ready.

Many Indians eat only vegetables and seafood, cooked with fresh spices. Rice or bread is served with every meal. Indian breads are round and flat. The most usual bread to have with a meal is chapati.

Eating the meal.

A very popular dish is Tandoori. Tandoori is
meat cooked in a very hot, clay oven called
a **tandoor**. Another favourite meal is dhal,
a thick **lentil** soup eaten with bread.

13

Clothes

sari

Indian women wear saris like these.

Most Indian women wear **saris**. Saris are usually made from cotton or silk. They can be very plain for work, or **embroidered** for special days. Some saris are embroidered with gold or silver thread.

dhoti

This farmer is wearing a dhoti.

Some men wear loose trousers called pajamas.
Farmers wear dhotis which are cloths tied round
the waist. In the cities many people wear clothes
like yours.

Work

tea bushes

Indian women picking tea leaves.

Most Indians are farmers. They grow rice, tea, sugar cane, wheat, fruit and vegetables. They can grow two **crops** a year in the hot, wet weather.

A quarter of all the tea that is drunk in the UK comes from India.

padlock

Repairing padlocks.

Some people work in **factories** and make cloth, computers, bicycles, cars and tools. Many people make and sell things from their own home.

Transport

rickshaw

A crowded city street.

In the crowded streets you will see lorries, cars, scooters, bicycles, rickshaws (three-wheeled bicycles for passengers or heavy loads) and people on foot.

Some people have to ride on the roof of this bus because it is busy.

Most trains and buses are so full that people ride on the roof. India's rivers are also very busy. Large and small boats carry people and **cargo** along them.

Language

४ वे वाटर मूवमेंट ४ गुना बेहतर

आसान किस्तों में उपलब्ध

ओ नि डा वाशिंग मशीन

Manglam JAWAHAR BHAWAN T. T. NAGAR, BHOPAL. 553134

Many different languages are spoken in India.

There are many different kinds of Indian people. Each group has its own **customs** and beliefs. Over 75 languages are spoken in India.

Both Hindi and English are taught in this school.

Hindi is the most important language in India but English is also spoken. Hindi and English are taught in schools so that Indians can speak to each other whatever their language.

Hindi is the official language of India.

21

School

writing
slate

Children at an Indian school.

Children go to school from the age of 6 to 14. They study Hindi, English, maths, history and geography. Some children write on slates with chalk instead of using pencil and paper.

basket of
tea leaves

This child works on a tea **plantation**.

Many children are too poor to go to school.
Their families need them to stay at home and
help farm.

Cricket is one of the most popular sports in India.

Indians are very keen cricketers. Children practise on the streets with a cricket bat and ball. Other popular sports are hockey, badminton, polo and football (soccer).

funfair ride

Funfairs are popular with many Indian people.

Many families enjoy going to funfairs in the early evening. The cinema is very popular. More than 70 million people go to the cinema every day. Indian film stars are treated like heroes.

Celebrations

Lighting the lamps for Diwali.

The different **religions** in India each have many festivals. Diwali is the Hindu New Year. The festival lasts for five days. Diwali is a festival of light and people light clay lamps in their homes.

flowers

paint

Celebrating the festival of Pongal.

Hindus also believe that cows are holy. The festival of Pongal honours them. The cows are washed, painted and decorated with flowers.

27

The Arts

Making a detailed design in metal.

Many Indians enjoy making beautiful things from metal, wood, stone or cloth. Their paintings and clothes use bright colours and detailed patterns. It takes time and skill to make such detailed patterns.

sitar

The sitar is played by plucking the strings.

The sitar is a famous Indian instrument. It is like a guitar with up to 26 strings. Sometimes its music is used for dancing to. These dances often tell old stories.

Factfile

Name	The full name of India is the Republic of India.
Capital	The **capital** of India is New Delhi.
Language	Most Indians speak Hindi and some English, but there are 75 other main types of language spoken in India.
Population	There are about 950 million people living in India.
Money	Instead of the dollar or pound, the Indians have the rupee.
Religion	Most Indians believe in Hinduism (which worships many gods). As well as Hindus there are also some Muslims, Christians and Sikhs.
Products	India produces lots of rice, wheat, tea, sugar, coffee, jewellery, clothes and machinery.

Words you can learn

ek (ik)	one
do (daw)	two
tin (dean)	three
namaste (nahm-as-teh)	hello
namaste	goodbye
shukrinya	thank you
mehabani seh (meha-bani-seh)	please

Glossary

bamboo	a tall plant with a long, strong stem
capital	the city where the government is based
cargo	things that are transported
crops	the plants that are grown and harvested
customs	the way people do things
embroidered	stitches used to decorate material
factories	places where many of the same things are made
lentil	a kind of bean
monsoon season	a time of very rainy weather
peninsula	land with water on three sides
plain	an area of open, flat land
plantation	a big farm that grows plants such as tea and coffee to sell
religion	what people believe in
saris	long pieces of cloth wrapped around the waist and shoulders
tandoor	dome-shaped clay oven heated by charcoal

Index